365
WAYS
to
SAVE
TIME
with
Kids

ALSO BY LUCY H. HEDRICK

365 Ways to Save Time
Five Days to an Organized Life

365 WAYS to SAVE TIME with Kids

Lucy H. Hedrick

HEARST BOOKS

NEW YORK

Copyright © 1993 by Lucy H. Hedrick

It is the policy of William Morrow and Company, Inc., and its imprints and affiliates recognizing the importance of preserving what has been written, to print the books we publish on acid-free paper, and we exert our best efforts to that end.

Library of Congress Cataloging-in-Publication Data

Hedrick, Lucy H.
    365 ways to save time with kids / by Lucy H. Hedrick.
      p.   cm.
    Includes index.
    ISBN 0-688-12700-2
    1. Parents—United States—Time management. 2. Mothers—United States—Time management. I. Title. II. Title: Three hundred sixty-five ways to save time with kids.
HQ755.8.H44   1993
640'.43—dc20   93-10220
                                               CIP

Printed in the United States of America

First Edition

1 2 3 4 5 6 7 8 9 10

BOOK DESIGN BY PATRICE FODERO

The author wishes to acknowledge many helpful suggestions from numerous friends, pediatricians, and parenting experts, and from the newsletter *Parents Together Primer*, Greenwich, Connecticut.

Preface

When my son was a toddler, I would bring him to his sunny playroom after breakfast each morning. He played there quite contentedly while I busied myself in the kitchen. All too soon, however, he lost interest in his toys and interrupted whatever I was doing. When I brought him back to his playroom and took a careful look around, I realized that there were probably too many toys strewn about the small room and that they were all too familiar. I decided to try a different approach.

I found seven shopping bags and divided all the toys evenly between them. I made sure each bag had a ball, a couple of stuffed animals, nesting cups, and perhaps a car or a train, and I hung them from nails or hooks on the walls. Each morning I would pour out the contents of one bag, and my son would amuse himself quietly for a long time while I got something done too. Why? I believe the toys held my son's attention because there were fewer of them and he hadn't seen them in a week. This playroom strategy became known among my friends as "Lucy's bags."

365 Ways to Save Time with Kids is filled with tips like this from actual parents, care-givers, and other experts. These tried and true experiences have saved time with children of all ages, from infancy through high school. The suggestions are helpful whether you're responsible for only one child or several, and whether you're married or a single parent. Moreover, the strategies are applicable if you work outside the home and use child care, if you run a home-based business, or if you're a full-time parent.

You might ask, is it really possible to save time with kids? After all, as every parent knows, raising them requires a lot of time. Furthermore, life with children is fraught with unpredictables—your newborn's feeding and napping schedule, your adolescent's moodiness, a sudden illness or injury. Enlightened parents, you could argue, learn to go with the flow.

True enough. And no one can really prepare for what's unforeseeable. But the mission of *365 Ways to Save Time with Kids* is to provide shortcuts and time-savers so *you'll have more enjoyable time with your kids.* This fun, low-stress time is achieved, I believe, by planning ahead and by being reasonably, but not overly, organized.

When your stress level is *lower,* your self-esteem will be *higher.* And as any pediatrician will tell you, less stress and more self-esteem will make you a happier, more successful care-giver. And since children often mirror the moods of the parents and adults who are close to them, if you're happy, the kids will be happy, too.

*   *   *

Note: "Lucy's bags" in the playroom worked for about a year and a half. By that time, my son had memorized the contents of each bag and began requesting Monday's truck or Thursday's bear.

Before You Begin

There are four organizing tools which I refer to throughout these pages. These tools, if used properly and consistently, will save you a lot of time. They are:

*A **Pocket Calendar:*** A calendar whose design you choose—perhaps a week-at-a-glance or one day per page—which goes everywhere with you.

*A **Pocket Notebook:*** A small, preferably loose-leaf notebook where you keep various checklists and that you take everywhere with you. The pages of your notebook are typically titled "Phone calls," "Errands," "Things to do," and "Things to write," plus any other task or list categories that relate to your life.

(*Note*: The above two tools are often packaged into "Personal Organizers." There is no right or wrong product. I recommend only that you use the tool(s) that work for you.)

*A **Tickler File:*** A group of file folders labeled 1 through 31, one for every day of the month, and twelve additional folders labeled for each month of the year. Your tickler file is where you put papers which you want to reappear on a specific date. For example, if Tim's school checkup is on the 10th of the month, put his school medical form in the "10" folder. If

Ginny must bring her check for the yearbook on the 17th, put the order form in the "16" file. Every day you pull out the file folder for that date, or the month's folder on the first of the month, and take action on its contents.

Permanent Files: A group of file folders for the papers you're saving for future reference (for example, immunization records, bicycle warranties, or a copy of your will). Your permanent files are stored alphabetically.

365
WAYS
to
SAVE
TIME
with
Kids

1

Sometimes parents have to invest a little extra time in the beginning to save some time later on. One patient mom I know buckles her son into the car seat, along with his three favorite stuffed animals. This indulgence saves her a lot of time because her son is cheerful and cooperative during the trip.

2

Peter, a stay-at-home dad with three kids, has written a list of emergency telephone numbers and photocopied it, one for each phone in the house. He placed each list in a small, inexpensive frame, to guard against tearing or sticky fingers, and mounted it beside a phone. The list includes numbers for the pediatrician, ambulance, poison control, hospital, fire and police, and his wife's office. He has also put *his* name, address, and phone number at the top of the list, to help a baby-sitter, in the event of an emergency, state exactly where she is.

3

Take "before" pictures of the interior of your home, especially the insides of closets and cupboards, before you renovate or re-decorate. The "old" photos are fun to compare with your spanking-new rooms and can be comforting to young children while the construction, chaos, and displacement are going on. Furthermore, this record of how to put things away saves lots of time when you move back into the refurbished spaces.

4

Inexpensive cassette recorders can amuse children for hours. Ask them to make a tape for a friend or cousin who lives far away. How about a "birthday tape" for Grandpa? Kathryn says the recorder is very much in demand at her house before Halloween, when her children record spooky sounds.

5

To motivate kids to get rid of outgrown toys and equipment, plan a family tag sale—or one with several families—and allow them to keep the money they get from their sales. Payoffs: You reduce clutter *and* teach your kids about salesmanship, negotiating price, making change, etc. "Always agree ahead of time," cautions my friend Jeff, "that unsold items are taken to the thrift shop or the dump. Nothing goes back in the house, except the profits!"

6

Pauline, a full-time working mother of two daughters, knows that certain music shows and open houses are more important to children than others throughout the school year. In September, she asks her daughters' teachers for the full year's schedule of events. She saves time—and minimizes hurt feelings—by asking which activities children traditionally expect their parents to attend and writing them on her calendar.

7

Save transportation time and money by booking appointments for several members of your family back to back. You and the kids can visit the dentist or eye doctor on the same afternoon. Be sure to bring a book to read or some easy "waiting time" chores.

8

Is yours a recycling home? Save time, and the environment, with clearly labeled receptacles for newspaper, mixed paper, and other recyclables. The containers don't have to be elaborate. Empty cartons will do. Let each child be responsible for gathering items in a certain category in preparation for weekly pickup or trips to the local dump.

9

Children of divorced parents needn't waste time packing up for visits back and forth. Let your kids keep some clothes, books, and toys at both houses. Other necessities to have at both residences: prescription medicines (a pharmacist can give you a second container) and homework supplies.

10

Sharon knows that her crawling daughter loves to explore purses, but often their contents are dangerous:

coins, medicines, or perfume that could be swallowed. Even car keys are sharp and dirty. To prevent accidents, Sharon keeps her own and others' pocketbooks out of reach but has a ''purse'' for her daughter with contents that are appropriate.

11

We live in a time when faster is better. Not always. A lot of people have rediscovered their ''slow cooker''—especially suited to those afternoons when a care-giver spends the hours before dinner driving the kids to their after-school activities. ''When we arrive home,'' says Christine, who drives her daughters to lessons after school, ''everyone is tired, cranky, and *starved*. But thanks to my Crock Pot, dinner is all ready.''

12

If you want to accomplish a family project—cleaning out the garage, raking leaves, or overhauling the attic—minimize complaining from your kids by letting them participate in the planning and timing. In addition, identify the reward that follows completion—for example, pizza and a video or a day off from chores.

13

I've been told by more than one working mom that changing care-givers is the biggest time-waster. "Keep up the relationship," says Audrey, an attorney who has always preferred a live-in care-giver for her two young boys. "Let her know that you care about her feelings, that she should communicate her concerns, rather than wait for disaster."

14

If you use a baby monitor, there's no need to run upstairs to check on your child. If your baby is awake or needs attention, you can hear her easily through one of these inexpensive intercoms. But don't get rid of your monitor once she gets older and graduates from her crib. A monitor is very handy to have when your child is sick in bed.

15

Kids can get a head start on lunch making—and parents can teach them the value of saving time in the morning—if they lay out their lunch boxes on the kitchen counter the night before and add any items which don't need refrigeration (plastic flatware, napkins, straws, banana, etc.).

16

A favorite pastime for a small child is playing in the kitchen sink. Frankie, a two-year-old, loves to stand on a chair and play with plastic cups and spoons in a few inches of soapy water while his mom fixes supper. And his mom says, "It's a perfect antidote to the 'five o'clock fall-aparts,' when little ones are tired, bored, and prone to tears."

17

Those wire hangers for Christmas tree ornaments are nasty if you prick yourself, and surely hazardous to a crawling baby who might swallow one. How about using colored yarn or ribbon—in a color to match your decor, in red and green, or in many colors? Let the younger children thread the ribbon through the ball or ornament loops and the older ones can tie them on the tree.

18

Restaurants that welcome children often provide booster seats. However, if the chairs have no arms, your youngster could topple over sideways. It's a good idea to bring along a bathrobe sash to gently secure your child and the seat to the back of his chair. Forget your sash? I've also seen an inventive maître d' secure a little one with a rolled-up tablecloth.

19

Judy, a mother of two in high school, has learned that *planned* outings with teenagers, often create too much pressure, unrealistic expectations, and disappointment on both sides. "And that's a *big* waste of time! *Seize the moment,*" she advises. "For example, you're driving your daughter home from team practice and spontaneously you stop for an ice cream cone. Or the car wash to benefit the youth center gets rained out, so you and your son rent a video and eat popcorn."

20

When you pack your young child's things for a sleep-over, you'll save time for you and reduce stress for her if you pack more than she'll need. Know that it's mostly in the packing that kids need to have familiar items—blanket, stuffed toy, night-light. Chances are they won't use them where they're going, but they are comforted by knowing the objects are nearby if they want them.

21

Parenting experts recommend calling a "time out," when you remove a disruptive child to another room, as an effective alternative to hitting. However, Maureen, a mother of three daughters, says that when tempers are flaring, including her own, she gives *herself* a "time out," and retreats to another part of the house to cool off.

22

Birth certificates, passports, your children's Social Security cards, certificates of baptism, etc., belong in a safe deposit box, along with other important family papers. However, make photocopies of these documents, and keep them in a file at home labeled ''Safe Deposit Box.'' The next time you need Johnnie's Social Security number, you don't need to go to your bank or vault. You can simply check your file.

23

A woman I know gives each member of her family a supply of large safety pins. When anyone takes off a dirty pair of socks, they pin them together. The socks remain pinned through laundry, drying, and putting away until they're worn again. No need to sort and match!

24

To minimize crankiness on long drives with your kids, carry an ample supply of snacks, lap toys, books, coloring books and crayons. Another stress reducer: individual, inexpensive tape players with head-sets.

25

Sally and Chuck owned two dachshunds before they had their first child. Their veterinarian recommended that they allow the dogs to sniff the new baby's clothing, powders, and lotions before meeting the baby, and to sniff the wet diapers after the baby arrived. Sally maintains that because the dachshunds were initiated this way, they're not jealous of the baby, just curious. Nevertheless, Sally and Chuck make it a practice never to leave their infant alone with the dogs.

26

With teenagers, having a weekly routine for who cooks supper when, and for whom, saves time and reduces hassles. A widowed father I know raised three children on this plan: Monday night Wendy cooked; on Tuesday, it was David's turn; Wednesday was Dad's special spaghetti; on Thursday Sarah cooked vegetarian; and on Friday night, they went out for pizza.

27

Kids can be anxious while waiting in the examining room for the pediatrician to come in. Bring along the book you were reading to them out in the waiting room.

28

What do you do with the packing list for Sally's overnight field trip that's two months away? Where do you put the medical checkup forms that arrive over the summer? In other words, where do you put papers that are pending? Instead of keeping them in a ''pending'' file, ''miscellaneous'' file, or just a pile, put them in your tickler file (see page 11) where they will reappear on the date when you need to take action.

29

My friend Ned fancies himself a movie director. Actually, he's the father of four and appears to be permanently attached to his video camera. When he cheers for David's soccer team, he's using the ''David tape.'' When it's Jill's birthday party, he's adding to ''Jill's tape.'' And so on. He tells me he's going to present these ''This Is Your Life'' tapes to the kids when they're much older. What a great idea!

30

The director of a local day care center told me her heart breaks when a child comes to school unprepared for a special event that's been planned for several weeks. "When forms and flyers come home with your child, your first stop is your pocket calendar," she says. "Make a note of what's happening when, so your child won't be the only one without a costume or Valentines or requested materials."

31

It's not pleasant to contemplate a situation when you would need your child's fingerprints, but you should have this record. Keep the prints in a safe deposit box. Many communities provide finger printing on a Saturday. Check with the Youth Division at your local police station.

32

My friend Janice with three small children solves the what-to-buy-for-birthday-party-gift question with what she calls the "gift of the year" plan. When she finds a suitable item on sale, she buys a dozen. Her three kids carry one of them to parties until her supply runs out.

33

Years ago I started what has become a popular tradition: a "Mom's Night Out" buffet supper at my house on a weeknight before Christmas. The menu is simple, we eat on paper plates, and my friends look forward to the event all year. They say it gives them a chance to catch their breath and catch up with their friends. Afterwards, they return to their holiday preparations with renewed energy.

34

"Parents who hire nannies or au pairs to care for their children should write out their specific instructions for the next day the night before, after the kids are tucked into bed," advises Louise, who has always employed au pairs. "In the morning, everyone is too rushed." The same holds true for sitters or other care-givers.

35

Mount an outdoor thermometer outside your child's bedroom window and encourage him to read it every morning. This will help him decide, and take responsibility for, what outerwear he'll need that day.

36

Do you have a well-stocked first-aid kit at home, in your car, or in your boat? Your local Red Cross probably sells them, but if not, be sure yours contains: assorted clean or sterile bandages and dressings, a triangular bandage in case you have to make a sling, packets of sterilized alcohol swabs for disinfecting a wound, antibacterial salve, syrup of Ipecac, Benadryl (diphenhydramine) capsules or elixir, aspirin, Tylenol (acetaminophen), calamine lotion, an ice pack, and dacriose or other similar type of eyewash. Check with your doctor or pharmacy for additional suggestions.

37

If your work schedule doesn't allow you to attend your child's recital, musical, or art show at school, try to arrange for a grandparent, aunt, neighbor, or baby-sitter to be there. Perhaps they can record it with a camera, video camera, or tape recorder.

38

Does your youngster have trouble concentrating? Does she turn a 45-minute task into two hours of drudgery? The ability to concentrate is learned, educators say, and it improves with practice. First of all, make sure that if she requires total silence, she has it. Second, start out small. Set a goal of 15 minutes of homework. Then stop for a 5 to 10 minute ''reward'' break before you ask her to focus on her homework again.

39

Give your child her own wall calendar, mount it near where she does her homework, and help her write in not only important events and family birthdays but also her homework deadlines—book reports, science projects, and the like. Giving children the opportunity to look at a whole month and take the long view will help them plan ahead and avoid doing assignments at the last minute.

40

Oven timers are good for more than cooking. Experts recommend that parents ignore quarreling between their children when they can, but when they have to intervene because one or more are getting hurt, separate the fighters and insist on some quiet, calm-down time measured by the oven timer.

41

To minimize long faces and cries of "Mom, I'm bored," Sharon has compiled a list of amusing pastimes for when she and her kids visit a friend who is childless and who therefore has no toys. Some of her ideas include: Hide some coins for a treasure hunt. Several pieces of wadded-up paper and a wastebasket make an instant basketball toss. Build houses with a deck of cards. Make a "city" using brown paper grocery bags standing ragged edge down; draw windows and doors with markers. Assemble 10 to 12 miscellaneous items on a tray for a game of memory, remove the tray, and then have the kids write what they can remember.

42

My friend Ann, an author of books on parenting and a mother of six, says that no matter how many children you have, parent-child time for each child is essential. For her, this is often achieved in the car while driving her children to events or activities. "Sometimes you can extend this one-on-one time by stopping for a snack or detouring into a store that's having a sale," she says. "But make sure it's a stop for your *child*, not for you."

43

When I enrolled my son in a summer nature program that was quite a distance from home, I made it my business to learn the names of other children attending from our part of town. After contacting their mothers, I wrote out a car pool schedule which saved all of us fuel and time.

44

Every day, more than 2 million children under age fourteen are alone before or after school while their parents are at work. Project Home Safe, sponsored by the American Home Economics Association and Whirlpool Foundation, offers several free publications for parents of children in self-care, including *Assessing Your Child's Readiness for Self-Care, Preparing Your Child for Self-Care, Finding Quality After-School Care for Your Child, Matching School-Age Child Care with Your Child's Needs, Tips on Self-Care for Parents and Children,* and *What If I'm Home Alone?* For more information write to Whirlpool Foundation, P.O. Box 405, St. Joseph, MI 49085; or call 800-252-SAFE.

45

Raising kids is rewarding but demanding, exciting but exhausting. Every once in a while, I have what I call a "write-off day," when all my plans go belly up and I have to let go of all I hoped to accomplish. That's okay. It happens to everyone. You can even have write-off weeks.

46

How do you get your child to bring home from school all that he'll need that evening? Have him write a master list—including assignment notebook, textbooks, papers for parents to see and/or sign, empty lunch box, backpack, eyeglasses, musical instrument—and post it inside his locker door. For the habitually absentminded child, enlist the help of a teacher or adviser.

47

How can working parents save time for the staffs of day care centers? "Label everything!" cry the care-givers. Replacing lost items wastes time, not to mention money. Chuck, as the father of two kids in preschool day care and two in an after-school program, is in charge of the family's laundry. He takes his marking pen in hand *before* a piece of clothing goes in the washer. Both centers love him!

48

What do you do with all the artwork that your kids bring home from school? There isn't a refrigerator in the world big enough to display it all. Teach your children to use a three-hole punch so you can store some of their papers in large three-ring binders. When grandparents and other relatives come for a visit, each child has a ready-made show and tell. For anyone who is unable to travel, the artwork can be mailed to them.

49

Every child over one year must have a Social Security number to be claimed as a dependent on his parents' tax return. Call 800-772-1213 and request that Form #SS-5 be mailed to you. Then you must take the completed form, your child's original birth certificate, one other form of identification for your child (doctor, hospital, or clinic record), and your own identification to your local Social Security Administration office. Your child's card should be mailed to you within 10 days.

50

When your high school student begins to think about colleges, have her buy a box of file folders which she can label with the name of each school she corresponds with and where she can keep copies of her letters and any materials sent to her.

51

If you've set aside time for yourself, don't be distracted by the dishes in the sink. An illustrator who continues to paint while raising two young sons says that her level of self-esteem at the end of the day is tied directly to her success at focusing on that day's top priority. She has good self-esteem if she paints while her sons nap, and if she avoids getting diverted by other things that need doing but are much lower priorities.

52

''Zoo Hour,'' ''The Witching Hour,'' whatever you want to call it, it's that time at the end of the day when your child knows you can't provide undivided attention, and lets you know that nothing else will do. One enterprising nanny has created a ''Four O'clock Box'' of craft supplies that occupies her charges when she fixes their supper. The idea has proved so popular that the children suggest outings to search for supplies, such as smooth stones in the summer, chestnuts in the fall, and pinecones in the winter.

53

Rachel's motto is ''Have tape measure, will travel.'' Her four growing boys are constantly needing bigger sizes. She measures and writes down the pants lengths, sleeve lengths, etc., of their clothes that fit and then shops for bargains on sale. Thanks to her trusty tape, she avoids bringing home the wrong size.

54

In this era of too much to do and too little time, parents often choose to do at-home chores themselves because they can do them quickly, rather than teach a child to do them, which will take more time at first. But consider the payoffs from delegating chores to kids: They learn a skill, they learn responsibility, they learn that they have value as a member of your family team, and you make some time for yourself.

55

It's important that your family's mail, your kids' papers from school, and all the other papers that come your way in a day not be dropped anywhere and everywhere in the house. Every family needs a large in-basket which collects all this paper until it can be dealt with. Try to empty the basket once a day, but *at least* once a week.

56

In a moment of exasperation over his dawdling kids, one father said to me, "I'm going to write a book called 'How to Put on a Sock in Less Than a Day.' " With children, you must allow extra time. Estimate how long it should take your youngster to do something—and then double it. Make a habit of rewarding her when she completes a task with dispatch.

57

A group of mothers in Virginia discovered a way to reduce "morning mayhem": They take turns walking one another's children to and from school. The kids love walking with their friends, and on their "walking days off," the moms have a little more time to do something else.

58

Time spent practicing something is time spent well. Whether your child is learning to play the piano, rehearsing a part in a play, or getting used to a new computer program, he needs to discipline himself to practice in order to move from mediocrity to mastery. Remind your kids that the race isn't won by the fastest runners, but by those who continue running. Most important, let them observe *you* showing some self-discipline.

59

Don't run out of your family's prescription medicines. Place a reminder to reorder in your tickler file or pocket calendar 1 to 2 weeks before you'll need it. Also consider ordering your medicine in bulk, perhaps 2 to 3 weeks or months worth, if your prescription is not likely to change.

60

When your child comes home during school hours due to illness, remember to call your after-school center. Many a day care bus has waited outside a school, delaying its riders, as well as other children on its route, when in fact the child left school earlier with a parent.

61

As youngsters grow older, they stay up later doing their homework. However, if they lose a lot of sleep, they can lower their resistance and get sick, and that's a big waste of time. Vanessa and Jim offer their teenage son and daughter a very tangible reward—extra allowance money—for every school night that their lights are out by ten o'clock (they get up before 6 A.M.). Works like a charm. It's one of the oldest behavior laws we know: Anything followed by something positive tends to be repeated.

62

You'll save time and extra steps if you establish a diaper-changing place on the first floor, as well as in your baby's bedroom.

63

Lauren urges mothers who hire nannies to delegate as much as possible to them. "Find their hidden talents," she says. "If they like to cook, have them bake birthday cakes. If they like to sew, have them make Halloween costumes."

64

Adam and Sara hold regular family meetings with their four kids. Every Sunday evening, between dinner and dessert, they talk about the upcoming week, divide up chores, or plan vacations. Each week a different family member takes a turn as chairperson. "The main exercise of these meetings is learning to listen to one opinion at a time!'' says Adam. ''And concluding with dessert ensures a pleasant ending.''

65

In teaching your kids the value of clutter control, have them store—and provide containers for—their possessions off the floor. Clutter has a greater tendency to pile if left on the floor of your closet, basement, attic, garage, and so on.

66

Sandboxes should be covered when not in use to prevent cats and other animals from eliminating there. Their wastes can carry organisms that are harmful, especially to pregnant women. Children can be taught to cover their sandbox with a simple tarpaulin and elastic bungee cords at the corners. This is preferable to a plywood cover, which can cause splinters or accidentally fall on a child.

67

My friend Roger sees his son from a previous marriage twice a month. "The difference between a 'great weekend' and a so-so weekend is setting aside a chunk of one-on-one time, separate from my new wife and our baby. It doesn't have to be fancy," he says. "Sometimes we just shoot baskets for an hour."

68

Teach your kids how to avoid paying fines for overdue library books. Show them how to write the due dates on their own calendars. As soon as they're able to check out their own books, let them pay their own fines!

69

Help! Your cousins from Omaha just called. They're fifteen minutes away, they're on their way over, and your house is a disaster. To facilitate a quick pickup, have a "clutter dumpster" in every room. A wicker laundry basket, a large ceramic plant container, or a wooden toy box is just the place to stuff *temporarily* the Sunday paper, the baby's toys, or your pile of mending.

70

Susan is teaching her kindergarten daughter, Molly, to get ready for bed—brush her teeth, get undressed, put her laundry in the hamper, take a bath, and put on her p. j.'s—all by herself. Susan busies herself with several chores in her own room—sewing on a button, putting photos in an album, laying out her clothes for the next day—so she's near her daughter, but Susan resists the temptation to stand too close and oversupervise.

71

Birthday parties for youngsters can be fun or unmitigated disasters, depending on how well you plan. Jane, who stages parties for kids at the local YWCA, offers this credo: ''Always have one grown-up or teenager on hand for every three youngsters who attend, and be prepared with more games and activities than you think you'll need.''

72

Do you wish you had more time to spend with your spouse? One enterprising couple has carved out time to talk to each other while keeping fit: They've hired a sitter three evenings a week for just an hour. While the sitter feeds supper to their kids, mom and dad walk and talk together.

73

If you regularly bring home children's books from the library and subscribe to magazines for young children and teenagers, you provide an enriching alternative to television. When your kids are old enough to read to themselves, you gain time to do something for yourself.

74

Listen, don't just hear. Think about the time you waste by asking kids to repeat what they said or by thinking you heard, taking action, and then realizing you mis-understood. Listen *actively* and occasionally, take a verbal ''snapshot,'' that is, briefly sum up what your child said. For example, you might say, ''Let me see if I understand what you've said so far. . . . ''

75

Save time and possibly save a life: Learn cardiopul-monary resuscitation and infant CPR. Better yet, gather a group of your colleagues at work and ask your employer to provide this valuable training.

76

When my son was young but tall for his age, I could predict that his clothing size would be twice his age, that is, at six months he wore size 12 months, at one year, he wore 2T, and so on. I often saved money by buying his clothes on sale in advance. However, chil-dren grow so fast in the early months and years that once or twice, I found myself with a warm jacket in July or shorts in January. Shop on sale, but watch out for the change in seasons!

77

How do you handle telephone and other messages at home? Designate a Communications Center, the first place everyone checks for messages, perhaps even their mail. Also, make rules for the answering machine—for example, kids may listen to messages but may not erase them until a parent arrives home.

78

Moving to their new home was less stressful for Tim, Erin, and their daughters because before the movers arrived to pack and load their possessions, both girls packed their own ''open first'' box. When the family met the moving van at their new home, the girls were delighted to open the boxes of favorite items. Furthermore, they didn't waste time in looking for lost toys!

79

To save time doing laundry, read the ''care labels'' on garments, and only buy clothes that are machine washable (warm water) and machine dryable. To save time getting kids dressed, buy skirts and pants with elastic waists to make them easy to pull on and off. To save time changing diapers, buy overalls with fasteners in the crotch.

80

Save time and reduce the likelihood of tears and tantrums before the December holidays: Don't put presents for very young children under the tree until after they're asleep on Christmas Eve. The holidays cause enough excitement without having to look at a pile of unopened gifts.

81

Child Care Action Campaign, a national child-care advocacy group, publishes 28 guides including *Finding Good Child Care—A Checklist* and *Speaking with Your Employer about Child Care Assistance.* You can receive up to three guides free by sending an SASE to CCAC, 330 Seventh Avenue, 17th floor, New York, NY 10001, or join (the annual membership fee is $25) and receive any of the 28 guides, plus a bimonthly newsletter.

82

Dividing children's visits between divorced parents during the holidays can be an emotional trauma. Resolve to reduce the stress this year: Start by asking your kids where they would like to be and when. Parents may have restrictions based on work and/or travel. Present a few alternatives. Some families establish new traditions at the outset of a separation: for example, Thanksgiving with mom, Christmas with dad; or Christmas Eve with dad, Christmas day with mom. You may choose a plan that alternates every other year. Whatever solution you come up with, let the kids have a vote.

83

To encourage our young son to pick up his toys and put them away, his father and I said, "You're the boss. Tell us how we can help you." Then he would delegate, for example, the blocks to dad, the cars to mom, and the soldiers to himself. Putting him in charge took the emphasis away from ending his playtime.

84

If you want your kids to be independent and make their own breakfasts in the morning, store cereals and cups and dishes in cupboards under the counter where they can reach them.

85

Moving can be traumatic for children. Charlie and Allison chose *not* to drag their daughters around while looking at possible houses to buy. Allison advises, "Wait till you're certain about events. We didn't show our kids their new home until we had the mortgage commitment."

86

Do your kids forget to bring their supplies to school? Help them get organized the night before by having a shelf, basket, or "out box" by the door. Have them write a permanent list which they can review before leaving: backpack, completed homework, papers that parents have signed, library books that are due, eyeglasses, pencils, pens, calculator, lunch or lunch money, and musical instrument.

87

Damage to skin from the sun is permanent and irreversible. Furthermore, who needs the aggravation of a painful sunburn? For a list of sunscreens that really screen your children's tender skin, send a self-addressed stamped envelope to The Skin Cancer Foundation, P.O. Box 561, Dept. SB, New York, NY 10156.

88

When you travel with your kids, keep a list of what you forgot to bring. From camping equipment to a piece of clothing to insect repellent, jot down the missing item in your pocket notebook and then file that paper for future trips.

89

Pre-teens and teenagers need guidance before they baby-sit outside the home. Confirm sitting jobs with the hiring parents first. Request that your teen tour the new home, review responsibilities, understand emergency phone numbers, and kids' routines.

90

When you have to redo a task because you didn't delegate effectively, you waste a great deal of time. When you ask your kids to help, you will save time if you define the following: 1) exactly what the task is, 2) why you selected them to do it, 3) the final deadline, and 4) how you will measure successful completion of the job.

91

Busy families can keep tabs on each other's comings and goings by using a desk blotter-size calendar on a wall in the kitchen. Each child's activities are noted in a different color of marker. Or you might prefer a sponge-clean type of calendar which can be easily revised and reused.

92

To encourage your children to help you in the kitchen, there are safe and easy chores that even the youngest can do. Little ones standing on a chair—at the counter, *never* near the stove—can be encouraged to stir a recipe, press the food processor buttons, and snap green beans. One gourmet dad I know lets his young son mix hard-cooked egg yolks (for deviled eggs) by squeezing them in a plastic bag. And don't forget a child's favorite kitchen task: eating the cookie dough!

93

When describing your kids, don't say "Johnnie was born organized but Susie's hopeless." No one is born organized. It's a learned set of skills, just like driving a car or playing an instrument. True, some individuals acquire organizing skills more easily than others, but anyone can learn.

94

Kids of all ages, especially children too small to shop for holiday or birthday presents, can practice the spirit of giving by offering family members the gift of time. For example, three hours of baby-sitting younger brothers and sisters, loading the dishwasher for a week, or doing another sibling's chores.

95

Bring home books from the library often, but to keep them from getting lost among the books you own, establish a library box in your family room, where they rest when they're not being read, and where you'll be sure to find them when they're due.

96

Professional organizers who advise parents on designing children's rooms and closets say that kids are more likely to put their belongings away if you take their closet doors *off*. In addition, provide low hooks and low hanging bars that invite them to store their clothes neatly.

97

Rather than storing sunscreen by the back door, keep some wherever your child gets dressed in the summer or while on a warm-weather vacation. Teach them to make a habit of applying sunscreen first thing every morning. Keep another bottle in your tote bag to reapply as the day wears on.

98

Many kids benefit from the structure of a weekly chart blocking out homework, chores, sports practices, etc. However, be sure to include free afternoons, allowance day, and other rewards.

99

Your pediatrician knows what vaccinations your child has had, but you should keep a record at home of shots and dates. This way you won't have to keep bothering the nurse when swim teams, camps, church retreats, and others ask you for this information.

100

Whenever there's a school holiday and I have planned on eight hours of uninterrupted time, I'm always disappointed. If you have a home-based business, be realistic. In September, note on your calendar all the dates your kids have off from school. Instead of being resentful of kids' interruptions, plan a day off for yourself, too.

101

A mother of six children told me, "My mission was to get my kids to do their own laundry, some by middle school, everyone by high school. I started their education by giving each child their own hamper."

102

To prevent soggy lunch-box sandwiches at lunchtime, pack bread and fillings separately. Children can put their sandwiches together right before eating.

103

College applications, essays, and financial aid forms are an enormous amount of work in addition to the homework your high schooler already must do. One caring dad I know helped his twelfth-grade daughter stay focused on her applications by accompanying her to the local library every Saturday morning. The father busied himself with his own projects while his daughter did her college paperwork. He's convinced that the regular appointment at the library allowed her to get the job done.

104

Plastic dish pans make terrific storage bins for small toys and craft projects. They're also easy to carry from place to place. The next time you see them on sale, stock up. You can't have too many.

105

How can you get more time for yourself? Stop picking up after your kids all day. Let there be *one* time of day when *everyone* pitches in to straighten up and put things away.

106

Two-income families often complain that their weekends are seldom relaxing, that they feel obliged to complete a long list of chores, and that they can't wait for Monday morning to return. Stop the weekend treadmill: Plan your fun and "downtime" *first*, and then try to let go of all but the most urgent to-do's.

107

Have your kids lost some parts to their Fisher Price toys? The company will send you a free catalog entitled "Bits and Pieces." Write to them at 636 Girard Avenue, East Aurora, NY 14052. Or you may request a copy by calling the Consumer Affairs Department at 800-432-5437.

108

How do you find baby-sitters when you're new in town? Check local bulletin boards, such as pediatricians' offices, YWCA's, and food stores. Also, ask about employment services at high schools, churches, and senior centers. Last but not least, ask other parents.

109

Are your children most demanding when you're on the phone? One enterprising mom I know found her daughter Shannon a small Sunday school desk at a yard sale and filled it with desk supplies and a play telephone. Now Shannon plays at her desk, coloring or cutting out pictures, while mom gets some work done, including phone calls.

110

Slowly but surely, study and organizing skills are working their way into school curriculums, but if your child is absent on the day the teacher explains how to set up a three-ring binder, your child has missed a valuable lesson. Don't leave these skills to chance: At the beginning of each term, ask to see your child's notebook and textbooks, and make suggestions for organization. How about subjects arranged in the notebook in the order in which they occur during the school day? Another child might prefer to have subjects arranged alphabetically.

111

Several of my friends swear by their tailor-made grocery lists. They have prepared a list of their regularly purchased items and organized it by the aisles of their favorite grocery store. Then they duplicated it, even going so far as to have them bound into pads. Then they and all other family members simply check off various items as they need replenishing.

112

To reduce the number of times you have to lift your infant or toddler out of her car seat, make use of drive-thru cleaners, restaurants with drive-in takeout, etc.

113

Pharmacists recommend that you clean out your medicine cabinet once a year. Throw away old prescriptions and over-the-counter medications that have expired. Medicines lose their potency after a certain amount of time. Check the label for the expiration date.

114

Many colleges today loan videos describing their campus and programs to students who may be interested in applying. Several families I know who have begun to look at colleges with their high school juniors bring along their own video camera when they visit campuses. Reviewing their videotapes later at home helps students remember the distinguishing characteristics of each school.

115

Sharon, a single mom raising two daughters, has "hired" her oldest, Didi, to play a board game with her younger sister, Adrienne, every afternoon at 5:30. This allows Sharon time to change out of her work clothes and start supper in relative calm.

116

Don't become the family alarm clock. As soon as your child can read numbers, buy him a digital clock and teach him how to use it.

117

When I ask men and women, "What's the number one thing that wastes your time?" they frequently reply, "Television." Diane and Lou, parents of twin boys, have resisted the TV trap. After the kids have gone to bed, they talk, listen to music, get caught up on desk work or read. And this regular quiet time together helps nurture their marriage.

118

Everyone needs a sense of ownership and privacy. Even in a large family, each child should have one place in the house that "belongs" to him—a desk, a room, a toy box—so each family member has a place to go and be alone, or keep things no one moves or uses.

119

You can minimize toddlers resistance to bath time by adding new tub toys. Use Styrofoam meat trays for rafts or an egg carton for a floating bus. An old beach bucket with holes in the bottom becomes a sprinkler.

120

Donna delegates grocery shopping to her children's nanny and finds this system saves time: She gives her nanny a blank check, plus her grocery store I.D. card. After shopping, the nanny puts the receipt under a magnet on the refrigerator so Donna can record her check and keep an eye on spending.

121

What do you do with those few leftover birthday hats, balloons, or napkins? Recycle them for a party for the household pet or some dolls or teddy bears.

122

You can save time and help your child's day care center if you bring a small duffel bag with a change of clothes, plus additional layers for outerwear. This bag should stay at the center.

123

Are you too exhausted to prepare designer cupcakes for your child to take to school on his birthday? Check first with the teacher to see if she would welcome a class project. If so, you can bake the cupcakes from a mix, but let the kids ice and decorate the tops themselves. Provide the teacher with ready-made icing, plastic knives, and sprinkles, candies, or marshmallows.

124

If you want to recycle your kids' outgrown clothes—to other children, to a yard sale, to the thrift shop—keep a supply of little price tags with strings. If the size tag has come off, attach a tag with the age when your child wore that particular article of clothing. Put the clothes in a box or shopping bag labeled with its destination.

125

If you put some fun into moving to a new house, you'll save time because your kids will pitch in and help. Many national moving companies have children's kits, including special labels, stickers, story books, and clever post-move ideas for creating play structures from large cartons.

126

If you work full time, you can still participate in your children's school activities. Make a point of contacting the class parent at the beginning of the year. Discuss the limitations of your schedule and get first pick of dates to offer your help.

127

Linda, the director of an after-school program, advises working parents, ''Don't feel guilty when you make mistakes. It's a big waste of time. Guilt lies in not trying and in not looking for better methods. If you make mistakes, it means you're trying to be a better parent.''

128

Ann and Derek have a son and daughter in whom they want to instill the spirit of giving at Christmas. On a Saturday in early December, each parent takes one child at a time to shop for the other parent. They meet at a favorite family restaurant for lunch, and then change shopping partners to complete the gift buying. It's become an annual tradition.

129

It's a plot! Grocery stores and others deliberately place candy and other temptations near the checkout counter because they know your kids are going to nag you to buy treats. How do you minimize cries of "Daddy, I *want*"? Don't shop when your kids are hungry or when the stores are crowded. Announce that you will present a lollypop reward in the car afterwards *if* they've been cooperative.

130

Give your baby-sitter clear instructions for TV viewing and point out alternative activities. Keep your shelf of craft supplies well stocked. One friend of mine was successful in inspiring the sitter to initiate projects when she sent her to the dimestore with some money and let *her* select projects she would enjoy doing with the kids.

131

Every family has a convenient storage place that's often overlooked. Store seasonal or seldom-used belongings under your beds. I bought a dozen cardboard boxes, or you may prefer plastic bins or sweater bags. Three to a bed, here is where we store hats, scarves, and mittens in summer or beach towels, swim goggles, and sunscreen in winter, as well as holiday decorations. I keep a diagram in the night-table drawer of the location and contents of each box.

132

When children are small, play dates with other kids are arranged by parents and care-givers. When they're old enough to place a call themselves, help them take some responsibility for their social lives. Write a list of their friends and phone numbers and mount it beside the phone. And encourage them to plan ahead and not wait until the last minute to find a friend to play with.

133

Your infant or toddler will be much happier while riding in the car if you invest in a dark green or blue plastic car window shade which shields children in car seats from the direct sun.

134

Do you complain you have no time for yourself? Bonnie, an author and mother of two, recommends making use of what she calls the ''hidden times'' in your day when you can grab some time for yourself. With the help of a reliable alarm clock and a caring husband, Bonnie carves out time for herself in early mornings and for a couple of hours on the weekend. ''Someone who's a night owl might find some 'hidden time' late at night, after the kids have gone to bed,'' she adds.

135

What should you carry in your stroller bag? Most caregivers remember diapers, a toy or two, snacks, and perhaps a sweater or jacket. In the warmer months when your toddler might skin a knee, include some packets of alcohol swabs and Band-Aids.

136

When you travel by car, train, or airplane with small children, you'll minimize their fussiness, and your stress, if you bring along some small presents to ease their boredom on the journey. A new book, toy, or coloring book will hold their attention longer than something old and familiar.

137

My friend Margaret, a musician, says it has always been important to have written goals for herself, ''even when, after my second child arrived, my goal was just to survive, one day at a time.'' Through long bouts of her kids' ear infections or days when it seemed they would never stop squabbling, Margaret would reread her goals and reassure herself that she would one day return to teaching and making music. And she has!

138

Pictures have a way of piling up without dates or subjects identified. Decide on a system for storing photographs and negatives. Most people feel more organized if they put photographs in albums soon after they're developed. Label your negative envelopes and store them in a box chronologically. If you're sure that you're never going to want another copy of Jenny on her first day of school, throw the negatives away. They're just more stuff to clutter your life.

139

Have you ever left your pediatrician's office and later recalled questions that you forgot to ask? Before your child's appointment, write a list of your concerns and add to it when another idea pops into your head.

140

Anyone who's lived with a preadolescent knows they sometimes lapse into "la la land," daydream, or tune you out. As I began to prepare my son for spending short periods of time at home alone during the day, I relied on *written* communication, rather than assuming he heard what I said as I was leaving. A quick note left on the kitchen table saying where I was going, the phone number, and when I'd return saved time and prevented misunderstandings.

141

Reading aloud to your child before bed shouldn't be the only time for this activity. Educators recommend it as a beginning for the idea of homework. Especially appropriate in families where older brothers and sisters already have homework, sit down with your younger ones and read aloud so they can feel like they're doing their assignment.

142

Your child's transition to college may go more smoothly if he's had some previous experience living away from home. One option is sleep-away camp in summer. You will need to consider whether your child will benefit from a highly structured program versus less structured. Is the camp accredited by the American Camping Association? What is the counselor-camper ratio? What are your health and safety issues? And most important, does the camp offer activities your child enjoys?

143

Don't wait for a cupboard crisis. When you're down to one package of macaroni and cheese, for example, stock up! Furthermore, teach *everyone* to write on the grocery list. (It's *not* just mom's job!) This goes for notebook paper and other school supplies as well.

144

Experts advise parents to acknowledge your kids' good deeds with lots of verbal praise. They also allow that sometimes it's all right to offer a material reward, especially when the offer is presented as a challenge: "If you and your sister can play peacefully this afternoon, I'll give you a present." The reward need not be candy. Kids are often pleased to get balloons, stickers, erasers, magnets, metal buttons, etc. Be prepared. Keep a supply of these little items on hand.

145

You can have a less stressful restaurant meal with kids if you ask for a table by a window and bring crayons for coloring on paper place mats, or a favorite small toy. If your toddler gets restless and fretful in his high chair, you may have to take turns with your spouse walking with your child.

146

In delegating to your kids, remember to teach the whole process. Laundry, for example, has four steps: washing, drying, folding, and putting away. If you show your children how to do all the steps, you won't waste your time completing other people's chores.

147

Avoid bunk beds and complicated bedspreads, dust ruffles, and pillow shams. Your child will be more willing to make a bed with a fitted bottom sheet, a comforter (with washable cover), and a pillow.

148

Diane, who has a live-in au pair to care for her son, recommends that your care-giver have her own television and phone in her room. ''She will have more energy and enthusiasm for her job if she has a sense of privacy and her own space in which to relax—in short, her own life,'' says Diane.

149

Other parents frequently compliment Doug and Peggy on their two well-behaved young children who obviously listen to their parents. ''What's your secret?'' observers ask. Doug explains: ''Our hobby is our kids.

When we're not working at our jobs, we're spending time with them.''

150

If you take time to plan, you can do almost all the preparation work for dinner ahead of time. Maryanne works full time and has three school-aged children. She can give her kids more attention when she comes home in the evening by getting a jump start on dinner in the morning. She routinely cuts up salad, marinates meat, and cleans vegetables in the morning. Furthermore, she assigns her kids simple cooking chores to do after school, like putting potatoes, or a casserole, in the oven to bake, setting the table, or emptying the dishwasher.

151

After a long hot day playing at the beach or in a dusty sandbox, offer your child a shallow plastic dishpan full of cool sudsy water where she can wash off her sand toys. She will learn about cleaning up while cooling off. But don't allow her to play unsupervised near a bucket with even an inch or two of water. She could fall in head first and drown.

152

In later elementary school, my son spent more and more time forming clubs with his friends. Keep plenty of equipment on hand for club play, such as paper, markers, tape, and flashlights.

153

Don't waste time playing telephone tag. If your kids go to a day care center, know the office hours of at least one care-giver on the staff so you can call with your questions or concerns.

154

Save wear and tear on your nerves and your home. If your house is small, or if your child's birthday falls during a month when you can't count on playing games outside, consider renting a neighborhood community room for your child's birthday party. My son's most successful and popular parties were held at a civic center where 8 to 12 little boys rode their ''big wheels'' around a big room—a perfect way to work off steam indoors in December!

155

Are you an effective delegator? If you think there's room for improvement, try this exercise: Imagine you've been in a terrible accident and you're in traction in the hospital for six weeks. Ask yourself: Which two people at work will you ask to do your job? Who at home can do your jobs in the family? And in your community life, who will you ask to fulfill your volunteer commitments? This exercise will help you identify your most important ''to do's'' and cultivate your most reliable helpers.

156

Every parent deserves to sleep late once in a while, say Jonathan and Nancy, who've worked out their own equitable system: On Saturday and Sunday mornings, they take turns getting up early with their little girls. Furthermore, whoever gets to be lazy on Saturday sleeps late on Sunday the following weekend.

157

To start your high school child thinking about the larger issues of choosing colleges—urban, suburban, or rural campus, large versus small, liberal arts versus business or science, for example—whenever you travel, stop at a local college and have a look around. These unpressured visits in the early years will save time in decision-making later on.

158

Have your infant's diaper bag ready at all times, containing diapers, an extra set of clothes, wipes, a light blanket, and plastic bags. A two-foot square of clear plastic vinyl, or a piece of a shower curtain liner, makes a portable changing surface. Keep a clean bottle in the bag, with dry formula in it, or use it for water if you're breast feeding.

159

If you're a divorced parent who shares custody of your kids, make sure their schools and their friends know how to call both parents' homes and work places. This information should be submitted on the school's emergency forms every fall and on the forms for student directories.

160

Is doing homework with friends a good idea? Yes, if the assignment gets done. No, if the time required to complete it is overly long. Insist on a beginning and an end to a joint effort, ideally after other assignments are done.

161

When children are young, parents and teachers give them rewards for good behavior—a compliment, a hug, a treat. A more subtle concept is teaching children to set their own goals and then reward *themselves*—finishing a book report, followed by listening to music; an hour's worth of math homework, followed by a snack; finishing the science poster, followed by watching TV. This ability gives kids a sense of being in charge and helps them get their work done on time.

162

Does your pharmacy, dry cleaner, or liquor store deliver? How about your florist, hardware store, or pizzeria? You can save time by taking advantage of delivery services.

163

Are you overwhelmed by the paperwork that the government requires if you employ a nanny or other workers in your home? Save time and costly mistakes by calling Paychex, Inc., in Rochester, New York (716-385-7522). For a little more than your worker's salary, Paychex will pay your employee and handle all the withholding and government filing. A company that specializes in small payrolls, Paychex will charge you by the frequency of employee payments and by the number of workers. The cost of this service to pay a nanny once a week is typically $14 a week for payroll service and tax payments, or $9 a week for just payroll service (they will tell you when and how much to pay the government). Paychex operates in 87 locations nationwide and assumes full responsibility for accuracy.

164

Knowing where to get information saves time. If you have questions about raising your children, consult your local library, your pediatrician, your friends, your community mental health center, or the school guidance counselor. Another tip for new parents: When we brought our infant son home from the hospital, we called the nurse in the hospital nursery (who, after all, had just spent several days caring for our son) and received a quick and reassuring answer to our question.

165

Need more storage space in your kids' rooms? Stephanie Schur, founder of SpaceOrganizers, White Plains, New York, recommends shoe bags hung on the backs of doors. The individual pockets are ideal for holding shoes, hair ribbons, jewelry, belts, etc.

166

Praise saves time. When you compliment and thank your kids for jobs well done, or "just because," you draw them in, fuel their self-esteem and create a spirit of cooperation. Surprise your child with a note of praise in her lunch box or on her pillow.

167

Is there a more aggravating question on this earth than "What's for dinner?" To make deciding easier, Julie keeps a loose-leaf notebook where she chronicles her own version of "The 60-Minute Gourmet." Her pages are divided into menus for company, favorite recipes of her family, and a few pages for new recipes to try. To avoid too-frequent repetition or cries of "What? Fried chicken again?" she arranges the recipes in an order she can follow from one day to the next.

168

When one child skins an elbow, call the others around so you can teach them how to handle minor cuts and scrapes—wash, disinfect, dress. Enroll older kids in a basic first-aid course. If someone gets hurt, they'll know what to do.

169

If you don't have time to arrange your children's awards, news clippings, or school play programs in a scrapbook, save the most important papers in a file folder, one folder per year. Years later, if you or they want to reminisce, you'll be grateful that you saved these highlights chronologically.

170

If you pay a baby sitter $1,000 or more in a calendar quarter, you probably owe federal unemployment taxes. Don't ignore this responsibility as *you* will be liable if your employee files for unemployment. Also, check with your state. There are usually payments to state funds for unemployment, disability, or workers' compensation.

171

If two children sleep in the same room and share a closet, have two closet rods, each painted a different color. The colors can also be applied to bureau drawers, bookshelves, and toy boxes.

172

"Little ones who attend a playroom will adjust to their new situation more quickly and easily if they have a specific care-giver to go to each time," says Mary, the director of a playroom program. "Remember to give the adult any special instructions—formula, allergies to certain snacks, where you can be reached—but also mention any significant loves or fears."

173

Do you think you've child-proofed your home? Nancy thought she had eliminated all the hazards that might harm her toddler until she had a "safety audit" performed by two friends with whom she wanted to form a play group. "Ask a friend to walk through your house and yard," she says. "You can overlook potential dangers just by being too familiar with your surroundings."

174

Do you make time to exercise? It's possible to combine keeping fit with spending time with your kids. Parents and care-givers can add a child's bicycle seat and ride (everyone wear helmets, please!), or they can walk or run using one of the popular three-wheeled jogging strollers.

175

The best time to buy kids shoes is late in the afternoon after their feet will have expanded. This is especially true in hot weather.

176

When you leave your children with a sitter, your instructions should include more than your whereabouts and phone number. Remember to point out the locations of emergency numbers, a flashlight, and the first-aid kit. Explain the house rules, including eating, bathing, and bedtime routines, in front of your kids. And don't forget ground rules for the *sitter*: use of the telephone, having friends over, or any foods that are off limits.

177

Are you thinking of having your child fly on a plane by himself to visit a parent or other relative? Learn beforehand the airline's policy for an "unaccompanied minor." Ask, for example, if there is a change of plane, what will the airline do to help your child get to his next flight. Ask also what happens in the event the plane is diverted due to bad weather. You'll save time if you prepare ahead of time with your list of questions.

178

Just because your toddler no longer likes to be wheeled around the neighborhood in his stroller, don't give it away. On vacations, strollers can provide naps for younger kids while older ones enjoy more sight-seeing.

179

How do you get kids to part with the toys they don't play with anymore? Insist on a playroom purge before every birthday and Christmas. "When my daughter was small, we called it 'making room for Santa's gifts,' " says Margaret. "Now we require each child to fill a bag for a charity or thrift shop. No bag? No birthday."

180

Don't forget about toy first aid. When you buy a battery-operated toy for a gift, purchase the required batteries at the same time, and keep a supply of extras on hand. Save assembly instructions and warranties in a file. Have a box or drawer with items for toy mending, such as glue, tape, and a small screwdriver.

181

Resist the temptation to pack suitcases for your kids. Let them gather what they'll need for their trip themselves. Teach them to count the number of days and nights away, and to make a list of what they'll need. Also, send them to their destination with their packing list pinned to the inside of their suitcase or duffel. And be sure to include a laundry bag or pillowcase, so your child can keep dirty clothes separate from clean ones.

182

Car seats are the law in all 50 states for children up to four years. To save time in shopping, ask for a free copy of the "Family Shopping Guide to Car Seats." Send a self-addressed, stamped envelope to the American Academy of Pediatrics, 141 N.W. Point Blvd., P.O. Box 927, Elk Grove Village, IL 60009-0927, attention: Family Shopping Guide.

183

When you're raising children, don't sweat the small stuff. If you use your time to react to every little crisis, to put out every little fire, you'll never accomplish anything—except firefighting. Choose your battles. Save your energy and time for the ones that really matter.

184

How can parents encourage their kids to get their homework done? Doing the work is not negotiable, but you can involve them in the decision-making. Let your child establish a regular time for studying every day. Let her also choose a regular place to do it. Make sure you have the necessary supplies, and agree on "quiet hours" when the phone, music, and TV are turned off.

185

If you use several sitters, write out your basic instructions, and then save the list for next time you go out. Writing down your directions can save time and prevent misunderstandings. And this way your sitter can refer to the list after you leave.

186

"When your child is going to fly somewhere on a plane by himself, bring your address book with you to the airport," advises Angela. "You will be required to complete paperwork concerning where your child is flying from and to, as well as the names of several relatives to notify in case of emergency. Always prepare two additional pieces of identification, one for your child's pocket and another for his suitcase."

187

If you count on your child's nap time to provide you with a little self-time, you know that your child's need for a nap often depends on whether she's had fresh air. On a rainy day, put on some rock music and dance, play "Simon says," give the kids pots and pans for instruments, and have a parade. The kids will work off some steam and work up a little fatigue!

188

Do you write a to-do list every day, but a big part of Monday's list becomes Tuesday's list which becomes Wednesday's list and so on? Carrying over tasks from one day to the next is a sure sign that your lists are too long (not to mention that it's needlessly demoralizing). Be realistic. You're probably doing as much as you can.

189

Tom's family responsibility is grocery shopping. He saves money by buying meats, as well as other items, in larger, "family pack" quantities. However, since his four kids are all on different schedules, pursuing after-school activities and part-time jobs, he freezes meats and casseroles in individual portions. This reduces waste from leftovers.

190

Save time and reduce battles with your "Terrible Two": Let him choose, but limit the number of choices. For example, don't ask, "What do you want for breakfast?" Also, don't say, "This is what you're having." Say instead, "Would you like apple juice or orange juice with your oatmeal?"

191

If you hire your first nanny, or a new nanny, part of her orientation must be to meet your child's teachers, doctors, and any other program provider such as the swim coach, gymnastics coach, or music teacher. Doctors will not treat your children, nor will teachers release them to strangers they haven't met. Before your nanny arrives, make a checklist of introductions you need to give her.

192

To reduce your children's anxieties about moving to a new home, look in the library or bookstore for juvenile books that talk about relocating in ways your kids will understand. After reading a book with them, invite them to share their questions or concerns.

193

Does your child turn a 30-minute homework assignment into a 90-minute ordeal? Does your adolescent daydream in the shower while your water bill, and temper, overflow? Buy a portable timer. The purpose is not to pressure your child, but to make him more aware of the passage of time. Let your child select the appropriate interval, and let the timer's bell help him stay focused.

194

How can you lower your stress when you're feeding your brand new baby and your older child is jealous and demanding attention? Let your oldest feed the baby. By inviting brother or sister to hold the bottle, you're not creating bad feelings by pushing them away. And very often your oldest tires of the task and goes off to find something more fun to do. (Breast feeding? Invite brother or sister to play a music box for the baby, or if old enough, quietly read aloud.)

195

Is it time to get organized to choose a pre-school for your child? The National Association for the Education of Young Children provides a free pamphlet: ''How to Choose a Good Early-Childhood Program.'' Send a stamped, self-addressed envelope to NAEYC, 1509 16th Street, NW, Washington, DC 20036.

196

When you pay your child's day care center, save your receipts. You may be entitled to a federal tax credit of up to 25 percent, depending on your income. The credit is on expenses up to $2,400 for one child, and up to $4,800 for two or more children. Strict limitations apply, so be sure to check with the IRS or your accountant.

197

Who needs the stress and discomfort of a bee sting? To minimize insect bites and stings, dress your baby in solid colors (heat-reflecting white is best), and avoid using perfumed lotions, soaps, and shampoos. Also, be wary of giving your child juice or fruit outdoors.

198

Do you get "four o'clock diminishing returns?" That's when while working at your desk, your shoulders slump, your eyelids droop, and you're probably reading the same paragraph over and over again. Save time by taking time off. Schedule a fifteen-minute break, once in the morning and once in the afternoon, and return to the task at hand with renewed energy. Furthermore, teach your kids that they'll get their homework done more quickly and more accurately if they take an occasional break to recharge.

199

In selecting your child's preschool, you'll save time if you limit your choices to the schools that are closest to your home. One mom I know, who visited a dozen, said she regretted selecting a school far from home. Not only did she spend more time transporting her daughter there and back, but her daughter made friends with her classmates who also lived far away.

200

If your child flies alone on a plane to visit the other parent, "choose flights and airports that are most convenient for your child's biological clock," advises Laura, whose son flies regularly to visit his father in another city. "Also, avoid returning home late Sunday night after a weekend away. Kids need time to get reacclimated and rested before school on Monday."

201

Prepare an identification card that your child carries in his or her backpack. Include your child's name, address, and home phone number, and parents' names and work numbers. Put the card and some coins for emergency phone calls in a sealable plastic bag. If you want your child to carry a house key, pin it to another place in the pack, away from the identification.

202

One couple I know whose budget is tight arrange a weekend alone several times a year by having their kids stay overnight with another family. Mom and dad go out for dinner but save on hotel costs by sleeping at home. Later on, they reciprocate by having the other couple's kids for a weekend.

203

Do you have trouble getting your kids to weed out their old toys? Consider this strategy: establish a "halfway house." Have them pack up into cartons some of the oldest possessions that they haven't played with in a long time. Put a date one year from now on the box and tuck it into a corner. If they don't touch the box before the date, give it to your favorite thrift shop. A halfway house works for clothes and papers, too.

204

When you're packing to go on vacation with your infant, put outfits together in clear plastic bags. Each morning you can simply grab two or three bags, rather than waste time rummaging around in the suitcase.

205

There are many household chores you can delegate to children which underscore the importance of putting things away: emptying the dishwasher, returning clean laundry, and putting away the groceries after shopping.

206

How do you handle your au pair's long distance phone calls and gasoline expenses? Several parents and nannies have told me their system: Give her a phone call allowance; any excess phone expenses are deducted from her wages. The same goes for gas for her car. And if the parents share the nanny's car, all drivers agree to return the gas tank at least half full.

207

The most frequently heard request from day care center directors to parents is "communicate, communicate, communicate." "In difficult economies, we find a lot of parents doing 'temp work,' which means they change employers often," notes Jody, a day care director. "Call your center or send a note with your child every time you change employers. Trying to locate you at your former job wastes time."

208

Get in the habit of saving items that you normally toss—bottle corks, plastic strawberry baskets, empty thread spools, cardboard rolls from toilet tissue—for a "rainy day box." When skies are gray and moods are glum, add some pipe cleaners, paper clips, scissors, and tape and invite your kids to assemble a creature or sculpture. While they're happily occupied, you can get something done, too.

209

Do you want to eat dinner as a family in relative calm? "Taking the phone off the hook helps," says Bill, father of four. "And stick to your routine," he advises. "Eventually, the spilling, crawling under the table, and tantrums go away."

210

When your kids get overly excited about who gets a turn first, choose a number between 1 and 10, and award the first turn to the child who guesses closest to the chosen number.

211

Don't give away your old typewriter! Even though many families now own personal computers, college applications must still be typed. To save time and to reduce frustration as your child tries to list four years of school activities on six lines, photocopy the application forms so your child can make a first draft.

212

To reduce the time it takes to get your rambunctious child dressed in the morning, lay out her clothes the night before. If she's particular about what she wears, offer her a choice between two outfits.

213

When raising kids, always have a "Plan B." If something goes awry with your first arrangements, be prepared with a backup plan. You may have to take a different route, but you can still reach your destination.

214

Save time by keeping a stock of individual snacks—boxes of juice, raisins and other dried fruits, and crackers—for your kids. Store them on a shelf or in a cupboard they can reach. Teach your kids to note items on the family grocery list *before* the supply runs out.

215

Roberta, who raised six children, told me, "Don't impose *your* lists on your kids. Let them observe you writing things down that you don't want to forget. Tell them that making a list makes you feel better than if you try to carry everything in your head. Then invite them to make a list of something they want to remember."

216

Parents complain that their child prefers the kitchen table to do his homework, even though he has a perfectly adequate desk in his room. Most children naturally gravitate to the family center, which is often the kitchen. If you want him to study in his room, move yourself, and what you're doing, upstairs closer to him. Wherever he studies, make it inviting, but with minimal distractions: a clear surface, enough supplies, a comfortable chair, adequate light, and a clock or timer.

217

A support group for nannies, or a sitter club, saves time and reduces stress because your child's care-giver can develop a social life apart from her work. Furthermore, when nannies or sitters make friends with each other, they arrange play dates for your kids, and they can back each other up if one of them gets sick. If your community doesn't have a nanny or sitter club, suggest that the local YWCA start one.

218

When you're cooking a recipe that can be frozen, double the quantity and freeze one batch. For the second meal, rather than duplicate your effort, all you have to do is put it in your refrigerator in the morning (or if need be, the night before) to defrost.

219

Keep a tweezers in your medicine cabinet, as well as in your first-aid kit, for removing a splinter, bee's stinger, or a tick. Understand the symptoms of Lyme disease and bee sting allergies.

220

If you're trying to reduce your spending, don't trim your budget so close to the bone that you have no discretionary funds. Pay yourself and your other family members a modest "allowance" to spend as you wish. Your budget will be easier to stick to if you don't feel like you have to sacrifice everything, including small pleasures.

221

Do you work hard all week and then face an endless list of errands on the weekend? One couple I know alternates doing these chores with one child, while the other parent relaxes at home with the other child. This solution provides one-on-one time with each child, as well as some downtime every other Saturday for mom and dad.

222

Do you have a system for getting rid of your children's outgrown clothes? "I go on a rampage at the end of every season," says Lynne. "I empty each drawer, or closet section, onto the bed and only put back what should stay. The rest I put in a box for a resale shop that shares the profits with me."

223

If you want to save time and money on redecorating when you're raising kids, use washable wallpapers and semigloss paints, which are easier to keep clean.

224

Did you know that videotapes, color slides, and most color prints have a limited life expectancy? If you want your precious family pictures to last for your grandchildren, have the photographer take a roll of black and white photos.

225

Procrastination is a big waste of time. Teach your children the skill of "eating the elephant one bite at a time," that is, breaking down a large project into smaller, more manageable steps. For a child's first book report, the bites will include: Select a book, read the book, outline or make notes for the book report, write a first draft, edit, and write the final copy. The same strategy should be followed by a high school senior planning a science project due at the end of the semester, a junior beginning to investigate colleges, or a ninth grader building scenery for the school play.

226

If you are changing sitters, save time by having the new one arrive one week before the old one departs. The new care-giver can learn her way around the community and your children's routines. If overlapping is not possible, have the first one make notes for the second. One young woman I spoke to wrote out 16 pages of notes for her replacement, which made the transition of care-givers very smooth.

227

If you want to start a play group for parents and kids who will meet in alternating homes, decide on the number and ages of kids, frequency and location of meetings, and agree on safety guidelines. In the case of a drop-off play group, the supervising adult should know how to reach one parent for each child, as well as each child's physician.

228

Too tired to cook? Keep a list handy of restaurants that cater to kids with crayons, kids' menus, etc. Consider meeting a friend and her children at one of these eateries. You'll get a little adult conversation and often your kids will be better behaved.

229

" 'Cool clothes' save time," insists Elaine, mother of two daughters. "I can only afford to buy my girls one pair each of name-brand jeans, which they launder and wear constantly, but we don't have any more battles about having to wear less expensive 'dumb' clothes."

230

Keep a list of rewards, that is, short breaks that you can insert into your day without feeling guilty, that will boost your energy, and give a shot to your morale. Your list might include: take a walk around the block, skim the sports section of the newspaper, close your eyes and meditate, buy some fresh flowers, play the piano, call a friend to chat, skip stones on a pond, play with your dog, and listen to music.

231

To prevent knocking over baby bottles in your refrigerator, save a couple of empty soft drink cartons to hold them upright.

232

Living with adolescent moodiness can be like walking a minefield: you never know when they'll explode. Keep *your* stress under control by not interfering too much. The parents I have most admired learned the fine art of keeping their mouths shut—especially helpful with teenagers.

233

When too many gifts arrive for your child at the holidays or for a birthday, put some away to be opened later. When your little one could use a lift, you can retrieve a box and say, "Oh, look, a special present from Grandma!"

234

Some teenagers have their first checking account when they get their driver's license; some when they get their first job. To get your teen comfortable with making deposits and writing checks, bring home some deposit slips, blank checks, and a register so he can practice filling them in. Insist that he sit down with the bank's manager to understand his responsibilities. Communicate in the beginning the consequences of overdrawing his account.

235

When you're traveling by car with your kids, stopping for lunch at a fast food restaurant is seldom

a "fast" experience. Save time and money by
bringing a picnic (you don't have to make the sandwiches ahead, just toss the ingredients into a
cooler). Then find a roadside rest stop or park
where your kids can run around.

236

Don't be embarrassed to take notes at your pediatrician's office when the doctor or the nurse is giving
you lengthy instructions. If your child has a high fever
or is quite sick, it's very stressful. Don't rely on your
frazzled brain to remember. Write it down.

237

The transition from office to home is difficult when
you work full time. To help separate your personal life
from your professional one, change into more comfortable clothing when you first come home. Parents
who work from home tell me a change of clothes also
helps them make the switch to family time.

238

You'll have more success getting your child to pick up his toys or put away the sports equipment if you ask her to do it at the end of the activity, rather than at the end of the day. And if a friend has been playing at your house, make sure she pitches in before she goes home.

239

Install an answering machine and ask your sitter not to pick up unless *you* are calling, or one of her friends. The people calling to talk to you can leave their message on your machine. Your sitter's job is first and foremost to take care of your kids, *not* to write down lengthy telephone messages for you.

240

To minimize the size and number of suitcases when you travel with your kids, consider shipping a few toys or out-of-season clothes to your new destination. You'll really save time when you fly if you can avoid the baggage claim. Have each member of the family bring a small carry-on duffel and send the rest ahead.

241

For a new diversion when the kids are cranky just as you're trying to get dinner on the table, let them play in the "sea": Open a large beach towel or old bed spread on the floor and toss out some bath toys—boats, ducks, or fish. Add some shells, if you have some, or perhaps a toy lobster or crab.

242

If you develop a repertoire of quickly cooked meals, you or your care-giver will be out of the kitchen sooner and have more time to spend with your kids. Whenever possible, involve your kids in the preparation. You're adding to the time you spend with them, as well as teaching skills and encouraging independence.

243

Do you have trouble getting your teen to be ready to go somewhere on time? Teens are frequently more co-operative for their *friends'* parents. Use this fact to your advantage: Form a car pool that involves as many other parents as you can. The more often you can take yourself out of the conflict, the better.

244

Save time while you reduce your pile of laundry. When your kids are small, never throw away an adult-size shirt. Cut the sleeves and even the shirt tails shorter, and your reject becomes an instant smock. Good for covering the clothes of little Picassos inside or backyard Annie Oakleys outside, several ''dirt shirts'' always hang on hooks by my back door.

245

Every Christmas, Shirley gives each of her children a tree ornament. They can choose to display it on the family's tree or put it away. It's understood the ornaments are theirs to take with them when they marry or live on their own.

246

A group of errands will proceed more smoothly if you include some *fun* stops along the way for your child. A playground or park is ideal in good weather, or the children's room of your library at any time. Another favorite stop when my son was small was the pet shop, or the pet section of the dimestore.

247

How do you save time in a family of picky eaters? "I prepare a basic carbohydrate entree—rice, macaroni, potatoes—and I add a variety of meats and vegetables," says Ted, bachelor father with three children. "Sometimes I'll hold out one ingredient for someone, but I never cook a special meal. There's always bread and salad, and nobody's starved yet!"

248

If you have a home-based business, keep it separate from your family life by having a business telephone number with its own answering machine. Instruct your kids and care-givers to use the home phone, *not* your work line.

249

Trying to be interested in activities that bore you wastes time. If you hate woodworking, tell your daughter you can't be counted on to demonstrate her new set of tools (but that you'll help her locate someone who can). If you're a klutz in the kitchen, tell your son you're happy when he pursues his own interests, but making sourdough bread just isn't your thing.

250

Help your kids manage their possessions by providing plenty of storage containers. Recycle shoeboxes, glass jars, even tin cans, as places to store their treasures.

251

Worrying, in my opinion, is the biggest waste of time. Furthermore, adult anxiety is contagious to kids. To call a halt to worrying, state as clearly as you can what you're worried about. Then ask yourself, ''What's the worst that could happen?'' Then identify three things you can do to prevent that possibility. And finally, take action.

252

Do you want to preserve the newspaper clippings of your daughter's sports victories or your son's role in the school musical? A copy will last far longer than the original if you photocopy it onto buffered (treated with an alkaline chemical) paper. Letters and other documents that you want to preserve should be stored unfolded in buffered folders.

253

If you work full time and family time is limited, make an appointment—just a short time each day to spend with your child—and then don't let anything interfere. (Take the phone off the hook!) It's not the quantity of time you spend; it's the quality. And more important, keeping your appointment—even if only for 30 minutes—builds trust.

254

Don't waste time dragging your preschooler around to investigate nursery school options. However, after you've made your selection and enrolled your child, make a pre-visit during the late spring. Plan to stay a couple of hours so you and your child can observe the variety of activities and ask questions.

255

Now that their kids are older and no longer believe in Santa Claus, Sharon and Bud take them shopping every October so they can write their Christmas lists. ''We take them to museum shops, hobby stores, and art stores so they get ideas beyond what they see advertised on television,'' Sharon says. ''Then, with lists in hand, Bud and I beat the December rush.''

256

There are specific things youngsters and teens can be permitted to do to vent their anger but that don't hurt anything or anybody: yell, stomp on the floor, or hit a mattress with a tennis racquet (a terrific de-stressor!). Other ideas: swing at a tree trunk with the cardboard roll from gift wrap, kick an empty carton around the backyard, or jump on and squash empty soda cans. Save time. Keep some items on hand in a "mad bucket."

257

No teens want their party to end by a neighbor having to call the police. In planning a party with your teen-agers, don't forget to include where the guests should park their cars and the parameters for wandering off out-of-doors.

258

Taking their kids to a crowded mall on the weekend is how many two-income families accomplish their er-rands. Remove the anxiety of losing your kids in the crowd by giving them a whistle to blow in case they get separated from you.

259

Do papers and permission slips from school get lost in your house? Teach your kids to put school notices and papers in one place—in a box or basket on a parent's desk.

260

Let your child use the telephone to schedule her appointments, whether for a haircut, the dentist, or the pediatrician. She'll gain confidence in talking to adults on the phone, and you'll have time to do something else.

261

Has your child been fully vaccinated? Booster shots are just as important as the regular shots for DTP, Polio, MMR, and Hib. According to the American Academy of Pediatrics, here is the recommended schedule for active immunization of normal infants and children:

2 mo. DTP (Diphtheria, Tetanus, and Pertussis), OPV (Oral Polio Vaccine)

4 mo. DTP, OPV

6 mo. DTP (OPV in certain geographical areas)

12 mo. Tuberculin

15 mo. MMR (Measles, Mumps, Rubella)

18 mo. DTP, OPV

2 yr. HIB (hemophilus influenza type B)

4-6 yr. DTP, OPV

14-16 yr. Td (adult tetanus toxoid, full dose, and diphtheria toxoid, reduced dose, in combination)

262

The best defense I've ever seen against an overrun of "the stuffies" (your child's collection of stuffed animals) is a rope hammock stretched between two adjoining walls, high enough so your child can get into his bed, and yet low enough so he can reach his favorite critter.

263

Many towns provide services for children who are at home alone after school before a parent returns from their job. These services save time by reducing anxiety—yours and your child's. A "Safe Home," for example, displays a removable sign that tells children that an adult is inside to help them if they're in trouble. In addition, your child should know how to call your local hot line in case they need help or information. Some community hot lines will even provide a reassurance call every day after school.

264

When your child is sick and you have to call your pediatrician, you'll save time if you can describe specific symptoms, such as vomiting or diarrhea, wheezing, abdominal pain, cough, headache, earache, runny nose, sore throat, stiff neck, unusual irritability or sleepiness or a rash. Take your child's temperature before you call.

265

Several families I know say family dinners turn from boisterous to peaceful when they turn off the lights and use candlelight. Little ones in high chairs are fascinated by a dancing candle flame. Let the older ones do the lighting using extra-long matches.

266

Readiness for trick-or-treating at Halloween means more than your children's costumes: Give each one a flashlight and a bag for their goodies. Accidents waste time, so rehearse children in safety procedures: Practice traffic safety, stay on well-lighted streets, only approach houses that have an outside light on, and don't eat any candy until mom or dad can inspect it carefully.

267

When making airline reservations for you and your baby or toddler, ask for seats in the bulkhead area of the plane where you'll have more room, and consider ordering a special kid meal that they will enjoy more than the usual adult offerings.

268

"It never fails," says Mary Frances. "When I'm racing against the clock, my children try to get my attention by misbehaving and compounding my stress. Conversely, when I slow down and spend time talking and listening to them, it saves me much time and energy in the long run."

269

Getting children used to going back and forth between two divorced parents' homes takes time. One amiable divorced couple living in the same town make it possible for their daughters' pet dog to visit Daddy, too. Now each home has dog food, feeding bowls, and a leash, and the girls are not forced to be separated from their beloved pet.

270

When you move to a new community, you have more to transfer than just your furnishings. Don't forget your children's medical, dental, and school records. You can aid in their speedy forwarding by providing the school or medical office with a preaddressed, stamped envelope.

271

For big holiday meals, like Thanksgiving and Christmas, let the kids leave the table when all the youngsters have finished eating. Now the adults can have some time to themselves before you call the kids back to the table for dessert.

272

''I tell new parents that a child is someone joining a family, *not* the focus of family life,'' says my pediatrician. ''To be a good parent, you have to be a person first. That means caring for your own needs and recognizing that they aren't totally subordinated to the process of being a parent.''

273

Infants of mothers who test positive for hepatitis B should receive HBIG (hepatitis B immune globulin) in addition to the schedule of required immunizations. Some members of the American Academy of Pediatrics are recommending the series of three vaccine shots for adolescents, as protection against sexually transmitted hepatitis B. Discuss this policy with your pediatrician.

274

A successful birthday party for children over three years of age requires planning. Aside from the obvious details of refreshments, games, and extra helping hands, be prepared with an arrival activity, that is, some kind of simple craft set up at a table so children have a quiet occupation until everyone has arrived. For example, take some free calendars, available at banks or hardware stores, and staple them to one end of a shirt cardboard. Let the children draw a picture at the other end. This craft is easy to prepare, easy to do, costs nothing, and the children can take it home!

275

The design and setup of a playroom or play area can determine if a child plays there. Space—pure, open space—is very important, psychologists tell us, in encouraging independent play. With lots of open "sky" and long "runways," a young pilot is not restricted from playing airport.

276

If there's a small job which you continually put off, try doing it first thing in the morning before you begin your usual routine. Completing the task can set the tone for the entire day—even though the day is only 15 minutes old, you've accomplished a very unpleasant chore. And be a model for your kids. Let them know why you're so "up" this morning.

277

When my son and I go on long road trips by ourselves, I always keep a large "identification card" in the front seat of the car. On a yellow lined pad I write our names, address, home phone, and the same for our destination. I include how to reach our immediate family, and also our allergies, blood types, physicians, and current medications. While I don't like to think of a policeman or other official needing my information, I feel reassured that it is immediately accessible and might save valuable time in a life-threatening situation.

278

Kids, just like adults, can use watching television to avoid doing something else—like their homework, for instance. Establish guidelines for weekly viewing, and spell out specific consequences for anyone who disobeys.

279

A supply of pipe cleaners can provide hours of fun for children, especially when traveling. Small, quiet, and clean, pipe cleaners can be formed into letters of the alphabet, jewelry, or animals.

280

Why increase your stress by worrying about your teens and alcohol? If you don't want your kids or their friends to drink what you keep at home, lock it up when they're very small as a part of your childproofing measures. "Even if your kids don't drink, a locked liquor cabinet helps them to keep their friends in line," says John, who prefers peace of mind where his two teens are concerned. "And this way, your son or daughter can blame the lockup on their parents."

281

"Don't store toys in a single, big toy chest," warns Stephanie Winston, professional organizer and author of the best-selling *Getting Organized.* "A child gets so frustrated digging to the bottom of the chest to pull something out that she'll fling everything else aside and leave it until the battle lines are drawn.''

282

Before kids are old enough to understand the importance of regular teeth brushing, they tend to rush through the job. Buy them a three-minute egg timer and encourage them to keep brushing until all the sand has run out.

283

When children don't listen and parents have to repeat what they say, it's a big waste of time. The best way to get your children to listen carefully is to listen to them. But when you have trouble getting their attention, get close to them, make eye contact, call the child by name, and gently touch them. They'll get the message and you'll save time.

284

Many pediatricians say your child will get fewer colds during the winter if you use a vaporizer in his room at night. A cold-water appliance is preferred because of the obvious safety hazard of hot water. However, stagnant cold water breeds bacteria and viruses. No matter which humidifier you choose, clean it on a daily basis. I take mine apart every morning and leave it to drain in the bathtub, and then reassemble it again before bed. As part of your routine, this doesn't require more than 5 minutes at either end.

285

Save time by taking some time off. You'll be more productive. As a family, make certain every weekend contains some free time for everyone—no homework, no chores, no dipping into your briefcase.

286

Don't change more than one important thing in your life at a time. If you're changing jobs, don't have a baby. If you're getting divorced, don't relocate right away. If you're moving, don't have surgery. You'll live longer if you take life's stressful moments one at a time.

287

There's a time in a child's life when she's too old for a day camp in the summer and too young to be employed. Solution? Volunteer work that provides some structure, teaches skills and responsibility, and gives work experience that will make her more attractive to an employer when she's old enough to apply for paid work. Ideas? Volunteer to help at a day camp, library, hospital, or museum.

288

Jerry, father of five kids, says Sunday night dinners are sacrosanct at his house; you can miss one only if you're sick in bed. At these meals, he says, "We fill in the family calendar as to who's doing what when, who will need a ride, who will need balsa wood for a project, and so on. If plans or needs change during the week, and they frequently do, we note changes on the calendar in red ink.'' How does he keep everyone from talking at once? ''We take turns sharing our plans, beginning with the youngest, and including Mom and Dad.''

289

You don't have to go overboard outfitting your new baby's crib. Start with the basics: a mattress; 2 fitted, quilted mattress covers; 2 flannelette-coated rubber sheets; 2 to 3 crib sheets; crib bumpers; and a couple of light blankets.

290

A new amusement for your child need not be a new toy. You can provide valuable parent-child bonding time if you regularly bring books home from the library to read aloud. When your children are older, subscribe to magazines for young people and continue to have library books lying around to occupy your kids while you get some time for yourself.

291

Martha, who works alongside her husband in the family nursery and landscaping business, recently lost twenty pounds and looks terrific. How did she stay on a diet while cooking three meals a day for her family? "I ate whatever they ate, but I used smaller dishes for smaller portions—a salad plate instead of a dinner plate, a teacup instead of a bowl."

292

Before you have your new baby, make sure you have a changing table or surface equipped with the following: mattress pad, two terry cloth covers (or towels), laundry bag, diaper pail with deodorizing lid, plastic bags for pail liners, deodorizing discs, diapers, baby wipes, comb, Q-tips, manicure scissors, and alcohol (for "cord care" right after baby comes home from the hospital). In addition, if you can mount a mirror so your baby can see it while on the changing table, you will amuse and distract an otherwise squirming baby.

293

In considering what floor coverings to buy while raising children, know that wall-to-wall carpeting or rugs will be warmer and perhaps absorb some of the noise, but bare floors—wood, vinyl, or tile—are easy to keep clean and are great for play.

294

If you have active children, ask your dentist what number to call in case of a dental emergency and add it to your emergency phone list. You can often prevent the permanent loss of a tooth if you get dental attention immediately.

295

"What is your secret to survival?" I asked Erin, who just had her third child. "Lower standards," she replied emphatically. "I keep reminding myself that our children are only loaned to us," she adds. "I'll have plenty of time for gourmet dinners and a House Beautiful after they've left the nest."

296

How can your preschool child know which audiocassette accompanies what story book? Match them by using sticker dots of the same color.

297

Lunch boxes are not only for carrying lunches. They can be used for small toys when you travel, for collecting things at the beach or park, or for holding Halloween candy.

298

You have many options in choosing where and how to bathe your infant—an inflatable baby tub, a large foam liner in a regular tub or sink, a hand-held hose, to name a few—but don't forget to take care of the baby-bather's back. Being out of commission with a strained back is a big waste of time!

299

Don't get rid of your baby's bassinet. In no time at all, this will be a bed for your child's baby-doll.

300

Did your family's picnic get rained out? Have it anyway—indoors. Spread out a very large sheet and eat lunch on the floor. For extra tolerant care-givers, kids love to push little trucks and cars around in cornmeal. Confine it to a roasting tray.

301

As the family photographer, Paul has, from the very beginning, created four albums, one for each of his three sons, plus one for him and his wife. "Whenever a new friend or girlfriend comes over, the boy wants to show her his album," Paul says. Is he always making duplicates of photos? "Hardly ever," Paul says. "I just take the pack and divide it four ways."

302

There comes a time when your children are old enough—assuming they are well-behaved and you trust them—to be left alone while you go away. "You leave plenty of food in the fridge and instructions in case of an emergency," says Linda, who has left her two college-aged daughters at home while she and her husband took a week's vacation. "For *your* peace of mind so you can relax on vacation, ask at least two trusted neighbors to keep an eye out."

303

Family newsletters at holiday time are controversial, according to advice expert Ann Landers, but for many people they save time, prevent writer's cramp, and allow you to stay in touch with many friends.

304

If you want to get out of the kitchen fast so you can play with your kids, modern technology can save you a lot of time. These gadgets are a must in today's kitchen: a microwave oven, a food processor, and an automatic coffee maker. Be sure to keep instruction manuals and warranties in one place where you can find them.

305

"With kids and organizing, you're *never* going to bat a thousand," says Lucille with a laugh. "Around here, it's a good week if the kids make their beds five out of seven days, if the dishwasher gets emptied without reminding, and if most of the sports equipment is returned to the garage."

306

If you want to prolong the life of your paint and wallpaper, make a house rule banning tape from doors and walls and give your child a large bulletin board and a supply of push pins.

307

If your child has difficulty remembering to do her chores, she may welcome a chart which lists them and provides spaces for her to check them off. Adults and children should recognize that lists are tools that save time, reduce stress, and free you up from the job of remembering.

308

Kids have biological clocks—peaks and valleys of energy throughout the day—just like their parents. Some kids are better in the morning and some in the afternoon. Don't try to change it; learn to work with it. If your son, for example, has trouble getting going in the morning, expect him to do his chores after school.

309

Locking yourself out of your car or your house wastes time. Make sure you have plenty of sets of car and house keys, label them clearly, and know where they are hidden. Carry an extra set of car keys in your wallet or purse or hidden under your car. Rather than have young children carry keys, which might get lost or stolen, hide house keys outside (but police do *not* recommend the obvious milk can, flowerpot, or "under the mat"). Have a specific penalty for failure to return the outside key after entering the house, as someone else might be locked out.

310

Need an inexpensive way to confine small children to your driveway and prevent them from running into the street? Use light but sturdy wire panels used as portable pens for pet shows, available at pet supply stores. Three panels across my driveway keep dogs and kids in the backyard.

311

Parenting experts suggest that when your child is late for the bus, let her stay home and miss school. But when single parents or two parents work full time, that's totally unrealistic. However, if you keep driving your child to school after she misses the bus, there's no *motivation* for her to reform. Forget repercussions; find an incentive. What will be her *reward* for good behavior?

312

Does your family use portable combination locks? Write down in a safe place the combinations for your bicycle locks, your locker at the fitness center, the cabin of your boat, and so on. If you lose a combination, it's very time-consuming to write away for the numbers and to possibly lose the use of your equipment.

313

My friend Susan says that her support group for women going through a divorce actually saves her time. Before she attended meetings, she couldn't get anything done because she was immobilized by her feelings of anger, frustration, and fear. "Now that I get my feelings out," she says, "I can move beyond them, do my job, and take care of my children."

314

To encourage the time-saving habit of writing things down, many schools provide students with notebooks in which to write down their homework assignments. When my son was in elementary school, a parent had to sign that day's page. In middle school, I've observed that the notebooks are provided, but many kids don't use them. Encourage your child to use a substitute that does work for him. My son prefers a small spiral notebook carried in his back pocket.

315

You can give your kids a lesson in botany and safety at the same time. Using an inexpensive guide to plants, identify all the indoor plants you have, as well as the trees and shrubs in your yard. Know which ones are poisonous if touched or swallowed and teach your children to recognize and avoid them.

316

According to the National SAFE KIDS Campaign, there are some 7,800 accidental deaths involving children each year. Many are preventable by using child-proofing devices that keep kids away from electrical outlets, medicine cabinets, cleaning supplies, open windows, hot water, and so on. An excellent, one-stop source is a mail-order catalogue called *The Safety Zone*. To request a free copy, call 800-999-3030.

317

Every parent should have a will. Discuss with your lawyer the decisions you need to make, including primary and secondary guardians, trustees and executors, talk them over with your spouse and/or other relatives, then tell your lawyer what you decided. Keep a copy of your will in your home, as well as in your safe deposit box.

318

To save time and smooth your child's adjustment to high school, have him take a class there during the summer before he enters. A class or two—for enrichment if not for remedial reasons—will still leave part of the day free for working and playing.

319

''Music hath charms to soothe a savage breast,'' wrote William Congreve in 1697. Dancing slowly to music can calm a fussy infant, listening to a tape or record of *Peter and the Wolf* can occupy and teach a preschooler, and listening to their own brand of rock can give your teenagers a way to have some privacy and independence.

320

Get started saving for college as soon as your children are born. The projected future costs of college are staggering, and the amount you'll have to set aside every year will be less the earlier you begin to save. Consider hiring a reputable financial planner to help you develop a plan.

321

Before you take off on a family vacation by car, make sure you're equipped with the following: working jack, road flares, spare tire, blanket, flashlight, and first-aid kit.

322

If you have a child with allergies, write and duplicate a list of foods and other materials she must avoid. The school nurse should have a copy, as well as scout leader, team coach, and the parents or care-givers of her friends. One organized mom keeps a small-size list of what her daughter is allergic to on the refrigerator for sitters and one in her daily calendar. This reminds her to tell the host parent of a party, sleep-over, etc.

323

I heard about a mother who was so pressed for time that she put her son in the bathtub with a toy boat on which she placed a cheeseburger that he ate while she read to him. You won't be surprised to learn that the little boy soon dissolved into a tantrum! It's a fact: The more we rush our kids, the more difficult they become.

324

To save time in sorting clean laundry or unpacking after a trip, assign each child his/her own color. This way they can quickly find their bath towels, sheets, beach towel, socks, and pajamas.

325

Car pooling works well if the other children in the group live close to you. If, on the other hand, you find yourself driving out of your way, are you really saving time? "Keep your driving distances short," advises Linda, a veteran driver. "It's awkward to release yourself from a car pool. Perhaps you and your child would be better served by some one-on-one time in the car."

326

If you're driving your car or recreational vehicle on your family vacation, don't plan a lot of full days on the road. "When we take out our maps and plan our vacation route, my son is in charge of calculating the distances in miles," says Charles, a divorced father who takes his two kids camping every summer. "Our rule of thumb is depart after breakfast and try to arrive at our next stop before lunch. That's usually not more than 200 miles a day."

327

When you're looking for a baby-sitter, remember to check references and to invest in a short visit with the new sitter in your home while you do a project in another part of the house or go on a brief errand.

328

When Ron and his family tried downhill skiing for the first time, no one knew what they were doing, everyone got cold and wet and was miserable. "Save time and limit fumbling," he now advises. "If you want to try something new with your kids, hook up with members of another family who have some experience.

You'll catch their enthusiasm while you learn the skills.''

329

Joan returned to full-time work when her twin boys entered kindergarten. How did she find the adjustment? ''Very difficult, but I learned to lower my housekeeping standards and streamline my actions,'' she says. ''We load the dishwasher once a day—after supper—the breakfast dishes just soak in the sink. We make our beds—or change the sheets—before we get in them at night.'' Now *that's* what I call ''letting go.''

330

Your new au pair will learn her way around your town more quickly if you give her a map and some written directions. Mothers who have spent hours driving their au pairs to schools, pediatricians, and gymnastics find that as passengers, the au pairs don't remember as well as if they were driving themselves.

331

Tell your kids that if they spend 10 minutes a day looking for things they've misplaced, they waste more than 60 hours a year. Some parents confiscate what's left lying around and demand small fines to get it back. Others label buckets, baskets, and boxes to make it easier to put things away. Whichever stand you take, set a good example: Put *your* possessions back where they belong.

332

If you have a child who's rebelling by choosing not to be organized, whose grades are slipping, and who refuses to accept suggestions from you, get some professional help. Organizing skills are too important to success in school and in life to let them slip away.

333

If you have adolescents who are demanding their own "space," a family vacation where your kids will meet others their own age is ideal. You're together as a family, but you're not on top of one another. Remember what vacations are for—getting away, relaxing, seeing new people and places—and that applies to adults and kids.

334

You can begin to instill good pickup habits in your youngster by breaking down a task into several steps. Instead of saying "Let's clean your room," begin by saying "Let's put your dirty clothes in the hamper."

335

When your sitter gets sick, be sure she sees the doctor right away. She should also have a flu shot in the fall.

336

Always be weeding out what you no longer use. When Harriet puts items away at the end of a season—hats and mittens after winter, beach towels after summer, decorations after holidays—she makes sure she doesn't put away what she knows she or her family won't use again. She puts the rejects in a shopping bag and takes them to her thrift shop in hopes someone else can benefit.

337

One of your child's regular activities of homework should be cleaning out his backpack and notebook. He should begin by emptying the pack completely. Put back only what's necessary. In addition, go through each section of the notebook and remove the papers that are no longer needed. Payoff: a lighter load to carry.

338

You can't avoid your baby's teething and its resulting discomfort, but you can make her more comfortable with special teething toys that can be refrigerated. When you're on the go, carry some of these toys in a small insulated bag, a Ziploc plastic bag with ice or a cooling pack.

339

Teach your kids about "Mommy time" and "Daddy time." Just because parents are at home doesn't mean they aren't entitled to some time to relax by themselves. Promise your kids play time with you—a game of catch, an outing to the park, building a castle out of blocks—as a reward for not interrupting while you read the paper or watch a game on TV. And then *keep your promise.*

340

Ordinarily, au pairs are off duty on weekends. However, she will get to know your family and its routines more quickly if she spends her first weekend "on duty." Let her observe your style of discipline and tell her the house rules in front of your kids.

341

Without a partner to share the child-rearing, a single parent is bound to build up some resentments, annoyances, and anger. Replenish your patience and energy. Find other single parents and pursue an activity that you do away from your kids. If you have limited funds, take turns watching each other's children so you can have some time alone.

342

To minimize back seat fighting during car trips, have one parent sit in the back seat. When you stop for gas or a meal, rearrange the seating.

343

Do you feel as if your family's schedule is so full during the week that there's no time to spend with your kids? Involve them in meal preparation, yard work, or errands *alongside you*—even for just a few minutes—and then you *are* spending time with them. This is especially true with teenagers who, come the weekend, prefer the company of their peers.

344

How can you make the most of parent-teacher meetings? Write a list of what you want to discuss. If you feel bringing out your list at the beginning might be threatening or off-putting, let the teacher begin the conference with his or her observations. Start off your remarks with a compliment, and then say, "To save time, I made note of some of my concerns."

345

Keep a list in your pocket notebook entitled "day trips." When you hear about a nature center, amusement park, or museum that others have enjoyed, make a note and then plan to visit during the next holiday from school.

346

To avoid juggling many carry-on bags when flying with an infant, put the contents of your purse in a plastic bag and tuck it in your diaper bag. Use your purse in your suitcase for holding toiletries or other small articles.

347

As babies grow, they will "talk" to themselves and play happily in their crib after waking, and mom or dad can catch an extra forty winks. Give your baby some crib toys which can be held in place with plastic shower curtain hooks.

348

Pauline, whose twin girls were born prematurely, recalls that she kept fit—and kept her sanity—by working out "between *constant* feedings" to one of several exercise videos which she played in rotation on her VCR. "Now that my daughters are in school, I still prefer my videos," she says. "I don't waste time commuting to a fitness center, and I can exercise faithfully, no matter what the weather."

349

Try to have a room or space in your house where you can leave out an ironing board and a sewing machine. Restitching a seam or pressing a hem is much more easily done if you don't have to set up the equipment each time.

350

Every playroom or area should have a "leave-out corner" for puzzles-in-progress, building foundations awaiting a roof, or awesome inventions. As children grow, play is their work, and the ability to finish a project in stages will serve them well in school and later on in their careers.

351

Parents of only children tell me that, especially as kids get older, vacations are more enjoyable for everyone if you bring along one of your child's friends.

352

"Simplify your life," says Steven, who was the custodial father for two sons who are now grown and on their own. "I changed jobs and moved so that I could live and work closer to my sons' schools."

353

When you hire a new sitter to stay with your kids while you go away on vacation, invite the sitter to visit and meet your kids beforehand. Write out your expectations and let them see it ahead of time. Include a daily checklist: bringing in the mail, newspaper, pet care, house keys, automobile instructions, etc.

354

When your kids have braces put on their teeth, they will be uncomfortable at first. In addition, they will be restricted from eating many of their favorite foods. Remember to ask your orthodontist if your child can have acetaminophen to reduce her discomfort, and what foods are acceptable.

355

Set an example by letting your kids observe you preparing for your morning departure for work the night before. Lay out your clothes and then assemble at the door (or in your car) your outerwear, briefcase, umbrella, and dry cleaning to be dropped off. Make it a family ''countdown to blast-off.''

356

In planning your child's birthday party, prepare a ''goody bag''—a small paper bag containing a few favors—for each of the guests. To minimize debris and loss, present a bag as each guest departs for home.

357

Make a decision early in the fall: ''*This* year I'm really going to enjoy the December holidays instead of run-

ning myself ragged and building up resentments.''
Plan *first* how you're going to ''feel the spirit'': hear
holiday music, entertain friends, be in church, or help
those less fortunate.

358

Make photocopies of everyone's identification: drivers' licenses, school I.D.'s, meal cards, library cards,
passports, and credit cards. Replacing lost I.D.'s is so
much easier when you have a record.

359

My pediatrician has observed that professional women
having their first baby are surprised when the systems
that work in the business world don't work at home
with a new infant. In reality, flexibility—or *not* making a schedule and sticking to it—is the cornerstone
of successful parenting. ''It's okay to plan,'' he says,
''but you must also agree *not* to plan.''

360

How do you provide a nutritious dinner when parents and kids are coming and going on different schedules? One family I know makes enough ''Sunday night casserole'' to be reheated in the microwave during the week. And since everyone is home on Wednesday evening, they enjoy an inexpensive Chinese take-out meal.

361

Do your kids complain, ''I'm bored. There's nothing to do,'' and you answer in dismay, ''You've got a toy store in that room of yours!'' Parents and care-givers should rotate kids' toys. Put some away for a while, and bring some others down from the attic. If toys are piled in a heap, it's too big and too much for them to deal with. Divide them up between several lightweight laundry baskets and start rotating.

362

Perfectionism is an enemy of saving time. I once knew a mother who, after her five kids had made their beds, went around straightening their efforts to make them ''perfect.'' This same woman always wondered why she had so little time!

363

If your child is going to travel with another family, you should provide him with a parental consent form. Write out that in the event of illness or injury, a physician or hospital has your permission to treat your child. In fact, if they have been unable to reach you, a physician or hospital will *not* treat your child unless they have written permission. Some parents, who are often away from home, have a ''permission to treat'' letter on record with their pediatrician.

364

A young girl was exploring on her bicycle and became lost. Admonished not to talk to strangers, she wandered several hours until, luckily, she found a familiar landmark. When your kids start to take off on their bikes, give them a local map, plus some identification.

365

"Children are like sponges. They absorb all your strength and leave you limp. But give them a squeeze and you get it all back." (*Reader's Digest*, February 1982)

Dear Reader:

If you have some proven ways to save time with kids, please let me hear from you. Write to me at: Hearst Books, William Morrow and Company, Inc., 1350 Avenue of the Americas, New York, New York 10019.

Thank you.

Sincerely,
Lucy H. Hedrick

INDEX

Tip numbers follow index entries.

braces, 354
buses, school, 311
businesses, home-based, 100, 248

calendars:
children's use of, 39
family activities tracked on, 91
recording school events on, 30
candy, 129
cardiopulmonary resuscitation
(CPR), 75
care-givers, 47, 63, 81
changing of, 13, 226
choosing of, 327
communication with, 207
errands and, 330
expenses and, 206
getting around town by, 330
hiring of, 108, 353
illness of, 335
instructions for, 34, 172, 176,
185
introducing teachers to, 191
messages and, 239
paperwork for, 163
payment of, 163, 170
privacy and, 148
support groups for, 217
telephone calls by, 206
telephone calls to, 53
television and, 130
vacations and, 353
weekends and, 340
car pooling, 43, 243, 325
cars:
care-givers and, 206, 330
car seats in, 1, 112, 182
distances traveled by, 326

drive-thru services and, 112
emergencies in, 277, 321
fighting in, 342
minimizing crankiness in, 1,
24, 133, 342
parent-child relationship and,
325
roadside stops and, 235
window shades in, 133
cassette recorders, 4, 24, 37
cats, 66
change, limiting of, 286
changing tables, 292
checking account, first, 234
child care, tax credits for, 196
child-proofing, 173, 280, 316
choices, limiting, 190
chores:
biological clocks and, 308
breaking down of, 334
breaks from, 198, 230
delegating of, 8, 54, 63, 64,
83, 90, 120, 146, 155, 205
kitchen, 92
lists of, 307
parent-child relationship and,
343
planning of, 12, 98, 305
remembering of, 305, 307
rushing through, 323
time for, 56
unpleasant, 276
on weekends, 106, 221
Christmas, 17, 33, 80, 128, 245,
255
Christmas ornaments, 17, 245
clocks, 116, 308
closets, 96, 171